Trapped in A Covid Bubble

by Giovanni Rosas

Illustrated by Julia Kosivchuk

TRAPPED IN A COVID BUBBLE

© 2021
Story by Giovanni Rosas
Artwork by Julia Kosivchuk

ISBN 978-0-578-86946-9

It was just an ordinary day at school, until it wasn't. When I was dropped off at school that morning, I didn't know it would be the last time I'd be there for quite some time. After school my Mom picked me up and told me school was closing for now because there was a virus called Corona out there. She seemed a little stressed and worried about it. Little did I know, this would turn out to be such a big thing.

That weekend was the St. Patrick's Day festival that my mom and I look forward to every year. They have carnival rides, a petting zoo, music, games and lots of fun. It was canceled due to this Corona virus. I was so sad that day since we couldn't go. This was just the beginning of many disappointments.

When Monday came we all had to start doing something called distance learning from home. "What? This was crazy." I thought." I had to get on a Zoom class meeting every morning to learn school. How was a teacher going to teach us behind a screen?" I didn't like these Zoom meetings but at least I got to see some of my friends.

Before Corona virus, I really liked being at school learning in the classroom having recess and playing with my friends. This made me start to feel sad inside. It felt bad staying at home all the time. I didn't even have a brother or sister to play with. My Mom needed to stay home to take care of me and help me with my assignments

We live with my Grandparents and during the lockdown it was my Grandma's birthday. We were going to have a family get-together and I was going to get to see my cousins and play with them. I was so excited until my Grandma said we had to cancel because of this Corona Virus. By this time it was more than a month and this virus still wasn't going away. What was going on? I didn't understand why this virus was so big and harmful? It didn't make sense why I couldn't see any of my friends or go anywhere. I then heard my Grandpa say he was going to stay home from work too until this virus calmed down. What? My Grandpa works all the time and now he's staying home. I couldn't believe it.

My family went for a daily walk together but other than that we didn't go anywhere. My Grandpa was the family grocery shopper and every time he came home he had to change clothes and we sprayed everything down with disinfectant.

Our weekdays were really long as my mom helped me finish my school work every day. Mommy was a little frustrated at times since she was trying to study for a very important board exam. I loved having my mom with me all day but we did drive each other crazy at times.

My school did their best to make us learning at home fun. They created a Lego Build-off contest that I was excited about. I ended up building a ninja dojo and won first place. One day, we all made cool signs and decorated our cars and did a drive-by parade for our teachers to show our appreciation. I started a ninja PE class on Zoom with my friends a couple of times a week to bounce around and be silly with my friends.

Time went on and I ended up finishing the rest of first grade at home. Boy, was this the hardest thing ever! Some days I didn't feel like doing any of my work. My Mom would get so frustrated with me. I really wanted to make her proud by doing all of my work, so I started doing my best work everyday. At the end of the school year, she got me a sweet present. That was so cool. I was happy to be done with school but at the same time felt disappointed that I wouldn't see my friends on Zoom anymore.

Summer vacation was finally here and the state officials said we could start seeing family and friends but to keep the gatherings small. They called it a "social bubble." I was really excited. The first thing I did was have a playdate with my cousins. We went out hiking and had lunch together. I felt so much joy. We had so much fun. I couldn't stop smiling and giggling. This was the best day ever.

f every summer, my Mom and I take a trip
nted to do this since we had been stuck inside
Iom passed her board and we definitely needed
id of her. We decided to drive down to the beach
feel so happy inside when I get to spend time
fun adventure together. The only weird thing
still around, we all had to wear masks to cover
Everyone looked so different. You couldn't see
ike walking ninjas. When we were walking we
ss the street to keep their distance. Everyone
each other or even say hello. "What was the

As the summer went on, we had small get togethers with family and friends. Still, it didn't feel the same. I was fearful at times by playing with my cousins or friends that I would get the virus. I couldn't get too close to them. This was really sad. I mean how could a virus be on their bodies? Everyone seemed fine so why couldn't I hug them?

Summer was ending and it was time to start school again. I really wanted to go back to school in person, but that didn't happen. The news said the Corona cases were going up and for our safety it was best to continue distance learning. "Oh gosh, not again! Distance learning from home?" I was not a fan. My Mom registered me with a homeschool program where we watched videos for every subject. I did learn a lot but it was so hard to sit in front of a screen all day. I just wanted to go to my school but I had no choice. I knew I wasn't the only kid doing this, and If I wanted to pass second grade I needed to stay focused.

The Corona virus kept getting worse, and we had to stay home again. I also couldn't see my friends anymore. "Here we go again, "I thought, "being all alone at home playing all by myself." It was sad to know that more people were dying and so many were sick. We had to cancel all holiday get togethers. I was sad honestly to not see my family on Christmas. My Mom reminded me we are still healthy and need to count our blessings. There were many people out there that lost their loved ones. I couldn't imagine my life without my Mom, family, and friends. Even though this Christmas was different it was still nice. On Christmas, my family and I had matching pajamas and played board games all night.

I can't believe 2020 is over. It felt to me like the longest year ever but we still had fun sometimes. It was a hard year but it did teach me some things. This year taught me to appreciate the important things like the love of my family. I appreciate being healthy and having close family and friends to see... and eventually hug. I try not to complain too much, and know that whatever happens we will get through this. I hope that 2021 will be a better year and we'll create lots of memories that I will never forget.

Made in the USA
Coppell, TX
04 April 2021